24 BLOG AND ARTICLE TEMPLATES FOR ASPIRING WRITERS

INCLUDES A FOUR-STEP WRITING PROCESS

D.M. BELL

Dedication

I dedicate this book to aspiring bloggers and article writers everywhere.

A Message from the Author

As an overly sensitive child, I learned the power of words. They can heal, and they can hurt. My obsession with words grew, and I began writing down my thoughts. The challenge was organizing my ideas, opinions, and views in a logical order.

If you're like me, this book will help organize your beliefs and make your writing flow. There are 24 templates. Each one offers a different approach.

The templates in this book have improved my writing and will do the same for you.

TABLE OF CONTENTS

TEMPLATES

Template 1: Basic Blog

Headline/Title

Keep the headline short (about 5 - 7 words). Make it an attention-getter. It should offer to entertain, educate, or solve a problem.

Links to your social media sites

Give your reader ways to learn more about you. Include social media links such as Facebook, Instagram, and X (formerly known as Twitter).

You'll also want to include your email address, a search box, and a share button.

Introduction

Write one or two short paragraphs and introduce your subject.

Post the main image related to your topic. Recommended size for images is 564 px. x 823 px.

Body

Persuade your audience by using personal experiences, facts, analogies, and statistics.

Break up the supporting paragraphs with…

- Images
- Graphs
- Charts
- Bulleted/numbered lists
- Videos
- Bold, italic, and colored text

Reminder: Keep your paragraphs short.

Offer a Bonus (Optional)

Add value by giving a free download. It's a great way to build an email list.

If you're an artist, share free coloring book pages. Authors can offer free eBooks. Food bloggers can post free recipes.

CONCLUSION

Close with some final thoughts and a "Call to Action". Ask the reader to leave a comment, answer a question, or click a link for further information.

OTHER POSTS YOU MIGHT LIKE

If you have other things you've written on a related topic, share the links. That could generate traffic.

ABOUT THE AUTHOR

Have an "About the Author" section/tab with your picture. Creating a bond with them is what blogging is all about. People buy and respond better to those they know and like.

Template 2: (#) Steps to…

This template is great for highlighting a step-by-step process for achieving a goal.

Title/Headline

Examples

"5 Phases of Accepting Diabetes"

"7 Stage Process to Quit Smoking"

"3 Steps for Beating Depression"

Introduction

Divide the topic into 3 - 7 steps to achieve. Introduce the reader to your process and explain the benefits.

Body

Outline each step.

> Step 1
>
> Step 2
>
> Step 3

Give the reader some added advice on how to achieve the desired goal and maintain their success.

Conclusion

Let your audience know that the process worked for you and that it can work for them, too. Remind the reader how they'll benefit from acting on your advice.

Template 3: Analogies

Use this template to make a complicated subject easier to understand. You can do this by comparing the topic's similarities to an unrelated subject.

Headline/Title

For the title, state the analogy.

Examples

"Life is Like a Trampoline"

"Owning a … is Like Being Married to…"

"Losing Weight is Like Becoming a Rocket Scientist"

Introduction

Lead the reader in with a story that introduces the topic.

Body

Outline the similarity in detail. Explain what these two unrelated subjects have in common. Let the reader know how the comparison helped you understand the topic.

For several related similarities, use an ordered list.

> Similarity 1

> Similarity 2

> Similarity 3

Let your audience know how the comparison helped you understand the topic.

Conclusion

Leave your audience feeling they've gained a better view of the subject.

Template 4: Current Events

Use this template to tie your topic or industry to a current event.

Headline/Title

Examples

"The Election and How it Could Change (an Industry, the Economy, Healthcare)"

"How will (new technology) influence (a specific industry)"

"The Lasting Effects of…"

Introduction

Summarize a current event/news story. Explain its connection to your chosen niche or topic. Make your target audience wonder how it will affect them.

Body

Include a paragraph or two addressing the challenges caused by this current event. Provide facts to back it up.

Offer tips the reader can use to avoid/resolve/minimize the problem(s) you've addressed.

Conclusion

Summarize the event, the impact on your niche, its effect on your reader, and how your tips can help.

Template 5: Frequently Asked Questions

People who have the same experiences also share the same questions? They're looking for answers. Use this template to supply those solutions.

Headline/Title

Examples

"7 Questions Every (New Mother) Has"

"5 Frequently Asked Questions About (Diabetes)"

"9 Top Questions Asked by Potential Employers"

Introduction

Summarize the topic. Let your audience know about your experience.

Body

In an ordered list, outline a group of commonly asked questions and answers.

- **Question 1:** Ask the question

- **Answer:** If there's a personal story behind the answer, share it. Let the reader know how you discovered the solution. Was it based on research, experience, or are the answers based on an opinion?

Continue to list the questions and answers until you've covered them all.

Option

Ask the questions in the form of a multiple-choice format. Provide the correct answers at the end of your post/article. With a multiple-choice layout, you can be as creative and humorous as you like.

Question 1

A)

B)

C)

Conclusion

Leave the reader with a sense of learning something new and a better understanding of the topic discussed.

TEMPLATE 6: GOAL SETTING

People with common interests share the same goals. They also share the same struggles in achieving those goals. Why not write a goal-oriented post/article to inspire them?

HEADLINE/TITLE

Examples

"Money Saving Goals and How to Achieve Them"

"Diabetes Management: The Importance of Setting Goals"

"How Setting Goals Help Me Lose Weight"

INTRODUCTION

Goal planning is the first step to success. Let your readers know they're not alone in their struggles.

BODY

If you have a success story, share your experience.

List of steps and tips used to reach the target.

      Step 1

      Step 2

      Step 3

Encourage your reader to:

Break the task into small steps and set a time for completion.

Celebrate each milestone along the way.

Find a friend who shares the same goal. (They can lean on each other.)

CONCLUSION

Recap your main points. Remind your audience that setting a goal is the first step in completing it.

Template 7: Helpful Checklists

Checklist posts are popular with readers. They give the impression of being direct, straight to the point, and without the fluff. Lists are great for helping people plan major events or to help get organized.

- Weddings

- Job searches

- Moving

- Vacations

- A new baby

Headline/Title

Examples

"The Ultimate Checklist for an Organized (Kitchen)"

"A Checklist of Supplies Every New Watercolor Artist Needs"

"The Must-Have Checklist for Expectant Parents"

Introduction

Explain why you wrote the checklist.

Body (the actual list)

- ✓ Item #1

- ✓ Item #2

- ✓ Item #3

- ✓ Item #4

- ✓ Item #5

Conclusion

State the benefits the checklist offers and how it'll make things easier for the reader.

TEMPLATE 8: HOW TO…

HEADLINE/TITLE

Examples

"Draw Impressive Cartoons for Fun and Profit"

"How to Bake an Apple Crisp the Whole Family Will Love"

"Learn to Become a Better Photographer in 5 Easy Steps"

INTRODUCTION

Start with a friendly overview. State the topic and share why you're so passionate about the subject.

BODY

Create a list of items, resources, and tools needed.

List step-by-step instructions to complete the task. Keep them simple.

Step 1

Step 2

Step 3

CONCLUSION

Give your words added value by including cautions, tips, and advice. Address problems readers may experience and how to solve them. End on a positive note and offer encouragement. If the new skill learned will open doors to opportunities, mention them.

Template 9: Lessons Learned

Use this template to write about a lesson you learned from an unlikely person, place, or thing.

Headline/Title

Examples

"Similarities Between Diabetes Management and Learning Piano"

"Healthy Living Lessons from My Bunny"

"How Getting Laid Off Increased My Self-Esteem"

Introduction

Give an overview of the person, place, or thing that taught you valuable lessons.

Body

Explain each point in a separate paragraph. What did you learn, and how did it improve your life? Did the lessons help you gain a better understanding of a situation?

If your points are short, use an ordered list.

Lesson 1

Lesson 2

Lesson 3

Conclusion

Remind your audience how they can benefit from what you learned.

TEMPLATE 10: MOTIVATION

Use this template to offer hope, inspiration, and strength.

HEADLINE/TITLE

Examples

"Calming Advice for Stressed-Out Divorcees"

"Emotional Eating: Here's How I Stopped"

"Diabetes and Its Emotional Challenges"

INTRODUCTION

Summarize the problem your readers are facing and let them know they aren't alone.

BODY

Share your wisdom and ways to deal with the obstacle/issue. Tell a personal story of your struggle and success.

You could also use

- A step-by-step process

- Individual tips in the bulleted or numbered list

CONCLUSION

Remind your audience of your success and explain how they will benefit from your advice.

TEMPLATE 11: MYTH EXPOSING

Use this template to write about a subject surrounded by misconceptions, false, or misleading claims.

HEADLINE/TITLE

The title should state the myth and your intentions of exposing it.

Examples

"The Keto Diet Exposed"

"Uncovering the 'Cinnamon Cures Diabetes' Myth"

"The Dangers of Vaping"

INTRODUCTION

State the myth, and why people still believe in it.

BODY

Use facts, experience, or a personal story to explain your view. Maybe you were the victim of a fraud. You could write a post to expose it and warn others.

Reason 1

Reason 2

Reason 3

CONCLUSION

Summarize the points and remind the reader why you believe the myth is false.

Template 12: Overcoming Obstacles

Does your target audience have a common obstacle they face? Is it one you've overcome? If so. Use this template to outline the problem and offer a solution to your reader.

Headline/Title

Examples

"Time Management for Busy Moms"

"Eating Healthy on a Tight Budget"

"My Biggest Weight Loss Challenge and How I Overcame It"

Introduction

State the obstacle you'd like to address and the effect it can have on everyday life.

Let the reader know they're not alone. Many others face the same challenge. Remind them that giving in to the obstacle won't help them achieve their goals.

Body

Give several reasons that can lead to this obstacle.

For example, what might cause a person with a chronic illness to give up?

Reason 1

Reason 2

Reason 3

Offer a plan of escape. Use unique ideas, strategies, tips, suggestions, and secrets (in the form of a list). You could also use a personal story.

Conclusion

Summarize the obstacle, ways to escape it, and how the reader will benefit by following your advice.

Template 13: Personal Story

People read to be entertained, educated, or inspired. If you have a personal story your readers could benefit from, why not share it? They'll feel connected to you and come back for more.

Headline/Title

Examples

"How I Overcame My Fear of …"

"My First Day at College: What I Learned"

"How Cancer Turned My Life Around"

Introduction

Start from the beginning. Give basic information. Answer (who, what, when, where, why, and how): the story began.

Body

Continue developing the plot. Share the lesson you learned.

Conclusion

Explain how your personal experience can help your reader.

Template 14: Persuasion

Use this template to motivate readers to change their point of view.

Headline/Title

Examples

"Sugar-Free Foods CAN Raise Your Blood Sugar"

"Don't Be Fooled by..."

"Why I believe the Keto Diet is Dangerous"

Introduction

State what most people believe as a fact. That shows fairness and understanding. Your audience is more likely to continue reading and learn about the opposing view.

Body

Begin with an opposing word.

- Yet

- But

- Nonetheless

- Ironically

- However

- Actually

Explain why you think the common belief isn't true. Use facts, evidence, experience, and knowledge to back it up.

Conclusion

Give your audience a feeling that they learned something and encourage them to rethink their position.

Template 15: The Secret's Out

People enjoy secrets. Share a little-known tip that will benefit your audience.

Headline/Title

Examples

"Secrets for Perfectly Roasted Chicken"

"Top-Secret Tricks for a Happy Marriage"

" 7 Lesser-Known Dog Training Tips"

Introduction

Give a summary of the topic.

Body

Explain why your tip is not widely known.

Share the secret in detail.

If it involves step-by-step instructions, use a bulleted or numbered list. That will make the text easier to read.

Conclusion

Summarize the secret and let your audience know how they can benefit from this information.

Template 16: Then vs. Now

Use this template for writing about changes. Specifically, ones that affect your target audience.

Headline/Title

Examples

"A Historical Look at Fashion"

"The Evolution of Cancer Treatment"

"Photography: Life Before Cellphone Cameras"

Introduction

Take the reader back in time. Describe how a process, tradition, technology, or way of life used to be.

Body

Discuss the changes and how they influenced society, an industry, or the quality of life.

Explain how these changes affected you. Were the changes good or bad or both?

If the effect was negative, how did you adapt?

If the change was positive, highlight the benefits you received.

Conclusion

Briefly review your main points. Focus on how the changes may have affected your reader. Remind them of the tips/benefits you've provided.

Template 17: Things to Do

Use this template to prepare the reader for achieving a goal or making an experience easier.

Headline/Title

Use different Tenses (before, during, and after) and Strong Adjectives.

Examples

"8 Important Things to Do During a Hurricane"

"5 Simple Things to Consider Before Changing Careers"

7 Critical Things to Do After You've Lost Your Job"

Introduction

Summarize the goal or action to be accomplished.

Body

Describe the benefits that the reader will receive by performing these actions. Lead into the list to follow.

List the Things to Do

Action 1:

Action 2:

Action 3:

Conclusion

Summarize your main points. Remind the reader what they can achieve by utilizing the list you've outlined.

Template 18: Tips and Tricks

Use this template to share tips, tricks, and shortcuts for a chosen topic, performing a task, or achieving a goal.

Headline/Title

Examples

"7 Ways to Beat Boredom"

"5 Tips to Improve Your (Photography) Skills"

"9 Tricks to Get Your Child to Eat Vegetables"

Introduction

Begin by introducing the topic and sharing the challenges you faced.

Body

Offer the suggestions in paragraphs or an ordered list. Back them up by explaining how you discovered these tips and how they helped you.

Tip 1

Tip 2

Tip 3

Conclusion

Summarize the points and value they offer. Encourage the reader to try your suggestions, so they can benefit, too.

Template 19: Solve a Problem

Use this template to address concerns your target audience is experiencing.

Headline/Title

Examples

"Learn to Crush Emotional Eating"

"Understanding and Fighting Depression"

"Building Confidence After a Toxic Relationship"

Introduction

Briefly describe a problem you'd like to address.

Body

Discuss the challenge in detail.

Providing a solution based on your own experience will catch the reader's attention.

If there's a secondary problem caused by the main topic, address it too, and offer a solution. Explain how they're related. Showing a connection will give a sense of unity to the article.

Conclusion

Summarize the problem(s)/solution(s). Encourage the reader to try to benefit from your suggestions.

Template 20: Success Stories

Use this template to write about a victory.

Headline/Title

Examples

"How I Achieved My Weight Loss Goal of 35 Pounds"

"Surviving a Toxic Relationship: How I Did It"

"What It Took to Land My Dream Job"

Introduction

Describe the success and its benefits.

Body

Introduce the reader to what helped you accomplish your goal.

Examples

- Did you lose weight? Was it a special diet or exercise program that worked?

- If you learned to accept a chronic illness, share how you did it.

- How did you master a new skill? Did you learn from a book, an online course, or a mentor?

Conclusion

Summarize your experience. Explain how the reader can use your tips and achieve success, too.

TEMPLATE 21: WAYS TO SAVE

Whether it's money, time, or energy, everyone loves saving. If you have a chosen topic and discovered savings techniques, why not share them?

HEADLINE/TITLE

Examples

"Save Money at the Grocery Store"

"Clean Your House in Half the Time"

"Quick, Easy, and Inexpensive Dinners"

INTRODUCTION

Give a summary of your saving tips.

BODY

If you have a lot of suggestions, present them as a list. Include detailed descriptions of each step (if necessary).

Explain how your ideas will help. For added value, give the reader an idea of how much money, time, or effort your tips will save.

Explain any drawbacks or problems they may experience while using your method. Give hints on how to avoid these issues.

CONCLUSION

Summarize your suggestions. Encourage your reader to uncover their own saving techniques.

TEMPLATE 22: PRODUCT REVIEW

If you're an artist, you can review art supplies.

If you're a photographer, review the latest cameras, photography books, or other products.

A mom who blogs about motherhood could review children's toys, books, etc.

HEADLINE/TITLE

Examples

"My Thoughts on the New (As Seen on TV Product)"

"Does the (Name a Product) Live Up to Its Expectations?"

"The (new iPhone): Is it worth the money?"

INTRODUCTION

Start with a brief introduction to the product. (Name, company, manufacturer, and its intended use. If you have an interesting story behind how you discovered the product, share it here.

BODY

- Summarize your expectations of the product and answer the following questions.

- Did you get the results you expected?

- Was the price reasonable?

- How was the quality?

- If the product included instructions, were they clear?

- Was it easy or difficult to use?

Add your ideas to the list.

PROS

List at least three benefits. (What features worked well? What made the product stand out? Was it better than other items you've tried?)

- Pro 1

- Pro 2

- Pro 3

CONS

List any flaws. (Was the quality poor? Have you tried other products that performed better? What else disappointed you?)

- Con 1

- Con 2

- Con 3

CONCLUSION

Give a rating and explain your decision. Here's the time to recommend alternative options if needed.

TEMPLATE 23: OPINION

Use this template for topics that create strong feelings and emotions. The point of this template is to make people reexamine their views. At least you've planted the seed with your clear and well-thought-out perspective.

TITLE/HEADLINE (Let the Reader Know What Position You're Taking)

Examples

"Does Global Warming Exist?"

"Don't Be Fooled by (Diabetic Miracle Cures)"

"Why I Don't Believe in…"

INTRODUCTION

Start by addressing a "popular" opinion. Respectfully share your viewpoint.

BODY

Explain why you don't agree with the majority. Use facts, experiences, or a personal story to get your point across.

If the explanation is long, give each point a separate paragraph.

For shorter points, use an ordered list.

Reason 1

Reason 2

Reason 3

CONCLUSION

Recap your viewpoint and defend your position.

Template 24: Fair and Balanced

Nothing's perfect. There are good and bad points to everything. Use this template to give a fair and balanced look at a controversial topic.

Headline/Title

Examples

"Things You Need to Know Before Becoming a Parent"

"Pros and Cons of a Vegan Diet"

"The Challenges and Benefits of Living in the City"

Introduction

Give a summary of the topic.

Body

Pick one side of the discussion and give details supporting that side.

Balance the article with a counterpoint to the original point of view.

You could also present both sides using bulleted or numbered lists.

List several benefits

- Advantage #1

- Advantage #2

- Advantage #3

List several disadvantages

- Disadvantage #1

- Disadvantage #2

- Disadvantage #3

Conclusion

Review both sides of the discussion, pick one, and explain why you've chosen it.

Ask the reader to think about the information you've given them and make their own decision.

Four-Step Writing Process

STEP 1: CREATING A STRONG HEADLINE/TITLE

A title should be around 60 characters (About seven to nine words). Anything longer than that will not show up in a Google search. The first two to five words are the most important in a Google search. Make them count by using keywords.

Use the title to grab the reader's attention. Its job is to let the people know what the post/article is about.

Will the post/article…

- Offer tips

- Solve a problem

- Answer a question

- Explain how to do something

- Provide a checklist

- Give advice

- State an opinion

- Compare the pros and cons

- Review a product or service

EXAMPLES

"How to Turn Simple Shapes into Cool Cartoons"

"7 Ways to Beat Lonliness"

"Save Time and Money Using a Slow Cooker"

TIP

Write 5 - 10 possible titles/headlines. Then, choose the best one.

STEP 2: TIPS ON WRITING A GREAT INTRODUCTION

Keep the introduction short (About 3 – 5 sentences). Outline what the topic is and why you're writing about it. Don't give away too much information. Keep the reader interested in learning more.

Explain what the article/post is about and why your audience should care.

If possible, end with a cliffhanger or a bold statement that leads into the main body.

EXAMPLES

- Tell a story

- Ask a question and make your reader start thinking right away

- Offer statistics, anecdotes, and personal experience to back up your main topic

- Open with a conversation (topic related) between two people. That creates a sense of eavesdropping, draws your audience in, and leads them into the meat of the article/blog.

STEP 3: THE MAIN BODY

This is where you deliver what the title promised. Discuss the main topic in detail. Ask yourself, did the reader come to learn something, be inspired, or be entertained?

Be generous to your audience. Offer them full answers, solutions, and strong advice. If you give your reader what they're looking for, they'll become loyal followers.

You get bonus points for adding something your readers weren't expecting. Do this by offering a unique angle, experience, or twist to the subject.

CREATE AN OUTLINE

Before you begin writing the main body, create an outline of the points you want to discuss. That will help organize your thoughts.

- Point 1

- Point 2

- Point 3

- Point 4

- Point 5

REVIEW THE LIST

Rearrange the list in a logical and clear order. The goal is to have one-point flow into the next, making your thoughts easy to follow.

WRITE THE BODY

Depending on the subject, you could write a paragraph for each point or use a bulleted/numbered list. Charts and graphs work well for statistical information.

The best option is to use a combination of paragraphs, lists, and graphics. This approach is the most visually appealing.

What you want to avoid is an endless trail of text, with nothing to break it up. Graphics, charts, and even subheadings can help.

STEP 4: CONCLUSIONS

Give your reader a pep talk. Ask them to think about how their life will change if they follow the advice in your post. Remind them that reading your words is only the first step in solving their problem or achieving their goal. They'll only benefit if they act.

Close with some memorable words, a quote, or a bold statement. Suggest a quick and easy way to put what they've learned to good use.

If you're writing for an online audience, include a call to action at the end of your conclusion.

The call to action should answer the question, "What next?"

EXAMPLES

- Click here

- Call us at

- Comment below

- Order now

- Buy now

- Share this post now

- Like us on Facebook

- Sign up for our mailing list

After you've completed the four steps, proofread your writing. Then, share it for the world to see.

www.ingramcontent.com/pod-product-compliance
Lightning Source LLC
Chambersburg PA
CBHW081253250726
48654CB00012B/1600